"Teamwork is the ability to work together toward a common vision. The ability to direct individual accomplishment toward organizational objectives. It is the fuel that allows common people to attain uncommon results."

— ANDREW CARNEGIE

WALKTHETALK.COM
Resources for Personal and Professional Success

To order additional copies of this handbook,
or for information on other WALK THE TALK® products and services,
contact us at 1.888.822.9255 or visit www.walkthetalk.com

Common Sense Ideas
for Building a Dream Team

The WALK THE TALK Company
1100 Parker Square, Suite 250
Flower Mound, Texas 75028
972.899.8300

WALK THE TALK books may be purchased for educational, business or sales promotions use.

WALK THE TALK, The WALK THE TALK® Company, and walkthetalk.com® are registered trademarks of Performance Systems Corporation.

Printed in the United States of America.
1 0 9 8 7 6 5 4 3 2 1

$10.95
ISBN 978-1-935537-67-0
51095>

9 781935 537670

Common Sense Ideas For

Building A Dream Team

Bud Bilanich
The Common Sense Guy

WALKTHETALK.COM
Resources for Personal and Professional Success

Introduction

Most people would agree that, with few exceptions, we are all born with five senses: sight, sound, touch, taste and smell. These senses help us navigate our way through the world. They bring us delight in small things: the turning of the leaves in autumn, an Eric Clapton guitar lick – or depending on your taste – a Yitzhak Perlman violin piece, the warmth of the sun on your face on the first day of spring, a favorite birthday dinner that your mom always made, the smell of warm bread baking. Those same senses also warn us when danger threatens: lightning in the sky, a police or fire siren, a hot barbeque grill, food that is spoiled and not safe to eat, a natural gas leak, etc.

However, I believe we all have a sixth and often underused sense – *common sense*. Your common sense can help you make the right decisions in ambiguous situations – but only if you use it. When I tell people that I'm "The Common Sense Guy," they often come back with the old saying, *Common sense isn't all that common*. I disagree! I think that we all have innate common sense. It's a natural gift – just like our five other senses. We don't always use it as well or as much as we should, though.

Fact is, most people *know* what to do in most situations because their common sense tells them. But it's also a fact that people don't always do what their common sense dictates for reasons such as: "it's too difficult and not worth the effort" … "it takes too much time" … "so and so might get upset with me" … "I don't know if I can do it." I've found that there are almost as many rationalizations for not following common sense as there are people in the world. And along with those rationalizations come scores of missed opportunities … and missed successes.

There are a number of simple questions you can apply to any task or situation that will help you better use the common sense within you and improve the results you experience:

Why? Where? What? Who? How?

I'll be using those very same questions to address a critically important issue facing most organizations today: How to get people working more effectively and collaboratively as teams – or, as I like to put it

How to build a DREAM TEAM!

So, get ready to take a common sense journey to better teamwork as together we explore …

- *Why* build a DREAM TEAM?

- *Where* can a team exist?

- *What* are the most common types of teams?

- *Who* do you include on a team?

- *How* do you build a DREAM TEAM?

Ready? Let's get going….

"Individual commitment
to a group effort - that is what
makes a team work, a company work,
a society work, a civilization work."

— VINCE LOMBARDI

Contents

Coming together is a beginning,
staying together is progress,
and working together is success.

— HENRY FORD

Why Build a DREAM TEAM?

Do you know the origin of the term "Dream Team?" The first time I remember hearing that label is when it was applied to the USA basketball team in the 1992 Olympics – the first year that professional basketball players appeared in the world games. The team was filled with legendary athletes and coached by a Hall of Famer, Chuck Daly.

The Dream Team was awesome. They won the gold medal, with an 8 – 0 record. In their eight games, they outscored their opponents 938 to 588. Their average margin of victory was 44 points. The final against Croatia was their closest game – winning by 32 (117 – 85). Coach Daly said, "You will see a team of professionals in the Olympics again, but I don't think you'll see another team quite like this. This was a majestic team." If you go that far back and you're a fan of basketball, I'm sure you'll agree. Those guys truly were majestic.

I bring up the 1992 Dream Team because it is a great demonstration of the power of teamwork. Every player on that team was either the best, or one of the two best individual stars on their professional teams. Most of them are now in the basketball Hall of Fame. However, they came together as one in the 1992 Olympics. They put aside their personal rivalries and concentrated on not only winning the Olympic gold medal, but also in restoring the USA to dominance in basketball.

The Dream Team is a perfect example of what can be accomplished by a group of individuals who unite and work together to accomplish a common goal.

So, to answer the question, "Why build a dream team?"

You build a dream team to accomplish extraordinary things that no one person can accomplish by himself or herself. You build a dream team to make your business more profitable … to better serve the clients of your non-profit … to help the kids at your school learn more so they can be better prepared for the future and more able to contribute.

Teams are powerful. The old expression **"TEAM – T**ogether **E**veryone **A**ccomplishes **M**ore" is true. At their best, teams make full use of the individual skills and talents of their members – creating a profoundly, unstoppable collaboration that truly makes the whole much greater than the sum of the parts.

It takes work to create a dream team, but it is work that's well worth it.

COMMON SENSE POINT

You build a dream team to accomplish extraordinary things
that no one person can accomplish by himself or herself.

Where Can a Team Exist?

In short – anywhere!

If you're like most folks, chances are good that you've been involved in a few "conference calls" with people in different locations – and hopefully some (if not most) of them have been fairly productive. These calls aren't team-building strategies per se, but they do demonstrate how a group can function well together even if its members aren't in the same location.

To be sure, it's much easier when the team is centralized in one place. There is no substitute for face to face conversation. But geographically dispersed teams can also work effectively. And in an increasingly global world, geographically dispersed teams are more and more common.

Recently, I had an assignment to facilitate a truly global team. I live in Denver. A couple of the people on the team were in New York, two in New Jersey, two in Brussels, one in Luxembourg, and four of the members were in Singapore. We set the calls for 9:00 in the morning US Eastern time. This was 3:00 in the afternoon in Brussels, 9:00 in the evening in Singapore and 7:00 in the morning in Denver.

We used the time differences as a team building exercise. We held a face to face meeting in New York to kick off the team. We spent quite a bit of time figuring out the best time for us to meet via the telephone. Our final decision was reached by consensus. Fortunately, the team members in Singapore are used to participating in phone meetings in the evening and were willing to schedule calls during their after work hours.

The decision on timing was a significant moment for the team. They were able to reach a consensus on how they would communicate … when they were going to meet by phone. This was an early success on which they could further build their team. As the facilitator, I often reminded them of the spirit of cooperation they demonstrated when tackling their very first issue: meeting time. This helped them get back into the consensus mindset when they were struggling over positional bargaining instead of consensual decision making.

Today, technology is making it easier and easier for geographically dispersed team members to interact with each other. There's plenty of software applications out there to help teams work better together. But there is a caveat: While software can link people to one another, it's only a tool. Teamwork is still a *human* endeavor. No matter how good the software, a team will not succeed if the members don't choose to work at making it succeed.

COMMON SENSE POINT

Technology has advanced to the point where it is possible for teams to include members from all over the globe. These virtual teams can be just as effective as centralized teams.

What Are the Most Common Types of Teams?

In my experience, there are four types of teams:

1. **Leadership** Teams
2. **Work** Teams
3. **Cross Function** Teams
4. **Project** Teams

Perhaps you've participated in one or more of these unique groupings yourself. If so, what was your experience? Was it a highlight – something that produced outstanding results like the 1992 USA Olympic basketball team? Was it a waste of time – something on which you spent an hour or two every couple of weeks with no real results? Or, was it somewhere in between?

Let's examine each of these teams…

Leadership Teams

I use this term to describe standing (semi-permanent) teams. These types of teams run an organization or part of a business and are typically comprised of mid-level to senior management personnel.

Some examples from this group that I've had the opportunity to work with include: manufacturing plant leadership teams, sales leadership teams, logistics leadership team, marketing leadership teams, HR leadership teams and enterprise-wide leadership teams.

Leadership teams typically assemble weekly, bi-weekly or monthly. They usually meet face to face – even when they are not co-located. In most cases, the purpose of these teams is strategic in nature. They set the overall direction for their parts of the business – ensuring that the units and departments they head up are in sync with, and contribute to, the mission of the organization. These groups lead and manage. Leading involves setting a vision and enlisting people to help them make that vision a reality. Managing is the nitty-gritty execution – setting general goals that will result in the achievement of the vision.

Work Teams

Work teams are groups of people who work closely with one another to reach specific goals. They can be sales teams, production teams, delivery teams, catering teams, whatever. Anytime a group of people comes together on a regular basis to accomplish something, they are acting as a team.

You probably belong to some sort of work team in your job. Some of these teams are highly interdependent. In others, team members do little more than coordinate their activities in order to get things done. It doesn't matter what type of team you're on. What does matter is that you do your job well while keeping the overall goal of the team in mind.

Cross Function Teams

These teams address one of the age old problems facing organizations: diversification and integration. Until the industrial revolution, there were very few organizations. Most people lived a subsistence existence – producing all of the goods they needed to survive. However, with the dawn of the industrial age, folks began working not just for themselves and their families, but also for organizations owned by others.

This model hit its height in the years following WWII when most of the "baby boomers" worked in companies that were large in size and ever-growing in scope.

In a nut shell, organizations exist because, in complicated endeavors, no one person can do it all. Multiple skills, talents and experiences are required. Therefore, they diversify – often by function, sometimes by product. However, as soon as you diversify, you face an immediate problem of integration – the need to get people and things that are inherently different moving together in the same direction. "Matrix organizations" are a structural attempt at addressing the diversification/integration issue. So are cross function teams. The basic idea is that cross function teams meet – usually on some sort of regular basis – to ensure that everyone stays focused on common goals and works together to achieve them.

Project Teams

These are some of the most common teams you'll find in any business organization. They come together for short periods of time to solve immediate problems or address specific issues.

Quality and productivity problems lend themselves to project teams.

"Six Sigma" teams, total quality teams, productivity improvement teams are all ad hoc project teams. So are meeting planning groups, product launch teams, product design teams, and other short term committees.

As I write this book, I am working with a project team that is designing a global sales meeting. Our charter is to design the meeting and manage it when it takes place. After the meeting, we will analyze participant feedback, and make enhancement recommendations for the next year's meeting planning team.

Project teams meet both face to face and virtually. Often, their members are separated geographically. They communicate via the telephone and meeting technologies. The thing to remember about project teams is that they operate for a finite period of time and then disband. Their "life" as a team may be a week, a month or two, or even a year – depending on the complexity of their task.

COMMON SENSE POINT

There are four types of teams that are most common in business today: leadership teams, work teams, cross function teams and project teams.

> The nice thing about teamwork is that
>
> you always have others on your side.
>
> — MARGARET CARTY

Who Do You Include on the Team?

Theoretically, this one is simple. You include everyone who needs to be involved so that the team will be able accomplish its task. Equally important, you *exclude* everyone whose participation *isn't* required. In actual practice, staffing a team isn't always easy.

There are lots of teams where people who don't need to be included want to participate because there is a certain prestige associated with team membership. And, there are some teams that are very important to the organization's success, but for which it's difficult to find members.

While both situations can be challenging, I have found that it's more difficult to cull potential team members than it is to find members for unpopular teams. Why? Because people who want to be part of a team can become disenfranchised if they are not offered the opportunity to join. A certain amount of finesse is required here. You need to explain why they weren't chosen to participate – presenting solid reasons that focus on the team's purpose and why the function they represent isn't absolutely necessary to the group's success. And emphasize that their time and special talents are needed elsewhere in the organization. Just be sure to avoid sending the message that they have nothing to contribute to "the big picture."

COMMON SENSE POINT

Membership on teams should be determined by answering one key question: Who has the knowledge and expertise necessary for this team to accomplish its goals?

How Do You Build a DREAM TEAM?

There are three components of a DREAM TEAM…

1. Clarity of **purpose**
    Common understanding of why the team exists
    The desired end-state the group is expected to achieve

2. **Internal** team **factors**
    Infrastructure
    Trust
    Spirit

3. **Relationships** with external constituencies
    Key constituencies
    Alignment
    Performance
    Image

I'll discuss each of these components in detail and show you how to build your dream team on the pages that follow.

> The welfare of each is bound up
> in the welfare of all.
>
> — HELEN KELLER

Clarity of Purpose

The first key to building an effective team is clarity of purpose and direction. As the old saying goes, *If you don't know where you're going, how will you know when you've gotten there?*

A team's purpose is sometimes referred to as its "charter" or "mission." The label doesn't really matter. Whatever you call it, you have to decide why you're in business as a team. It may be to lead and manage an organization or to solve a particular problem. Perhaps it's to coordinate efforts across functions in your company or plan a large and important meeting. Your purpose need not be complicated, but it does need to be clear and understood by everyone involved.

Here are some of the questions to help pinpoint your team's purpose:
- What is the objective for this team?
- What key issues will the team address?
- What will be the key activities of the team?
- What are the parameters and authority of the team?
- What are the team's key deliverables?
- What is the timing of those key deliverables?

Answer these questions and your team will be off to a great start

COMMON SENSE POINT

Dream teams clarify their purpose. They refer to it often as they go about their work. A team's purpose keeps it on track.

Internal Team Factors

You have to do a good job on the internal factors if you want to create a successful team. This is where most team development efforts focus; and it's very important for the group's success.

There are a few goals to keep in mind when building a DREAM TEAM

Everyone on the team needs to feel included and involved.

Everyone on the team needs to feel respected as a human being and valued as a vital contributor.

Everyone needs to know what is expected of him or her.

To meet those goals, you need to focus on the three main internal factors:

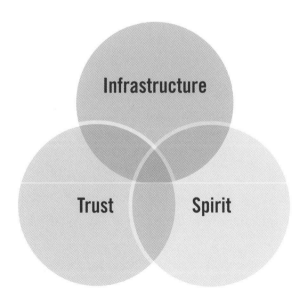

Let's look at each of these in a little more detail ...

Infrastructure

A team's "infrastructure" includes **Membership**, **Ground Rules**, **Leadership**, and **Rules & Responsibilities**.

Membership is one of the first questions that need to be addressed when you're kicking off a team. I always suggest that you think in terms of the functions that need to be represented if the team is going to succeed – not the people you want on the team.

For example, I work with a lot of leadership teams in the manufacturing sector. A typical manufacturing location has several functions:

- Production
- Packaging
- Quality
- Human Resources
- Environment, Health and Safety
- Continuous Improvement
- Finance
- IT
- Logistics

At some locations, a couple of these functions may be combined – at others, there may be more than those I listed. But you get the point.

Using the example above, the leadership team for this manufacturing site would likely have ten members – the site leader and nine functional leaders. The decision here is somewhat simple. The leaders of the key functions will comprise the leadership team.

Now let's look at a <u>cross function team</u> for a similar type of organization.

It's not uncommon to find communication and coordination problems between the production, packaging, logistics and quality functions at a manufacturing site. Therefore, if you wanted to create a team to address communication problems across these four functions, you would need representatives of each of the four functions.

You might decide that you want to have a mix of leaders and individual contributors on the team. A common solution would be to include one supervisor or manager – and one individual contributor – from each function. In this way, the team would benefit from having the leadership perspective as well as the "hands on" operating perspective. So, this team would have eight participants – a number large enough to have a variety of opinions and small enough to get some actual work done.

The same holds true for a <u>project team</u>. Let's say you wanted to use a team to plan and conduct an employee recognition day. In this case, you might want to have as wide a cross section of the facility as possible. At a minimum, you would want representatives of each function. It might also be wise to involve employees at different levels of the organization. So, this team might be rather large – two members from each function, at least one individual contributor, and representatives of the various levels of management.

A large team here is a good idea because you can break the work into sub teams. One sub team might focus on the program, another on the refreshments, another on entertainment. In this way all team members will be able to be active participants.

Clearly, every team will have its own unique membership requirements depending on its purpose. I've presented examples to show you how you want to think about team membership decisions – not to propose steadfast rules. You will need to determine what's best for you and your organization – using common sense as your primary guide.

COMMON SENSE POINT

Make sure you have representation from all of the functions that need to have input to the team and its success.

"Work and self-worth
are the two factors that interact with
each other and tend to increase
the strong sense of pride found
in superior work teams.
When people do something
of obvious worth, they feel a strong
sense of personal worth."

— DENNIS KINLAW

Ground rules are also important for any team. They are agreements on how the team will work together.

There are two types of team ground rules: behavioral and procedural.

Behavioral ground rules define how team members will interact with one another, interpersonally. Procedural ground rules highlight the mechanics of the how the team is going to work together.

> *Note*: For lists of typical behavioral and procedural ground rules, go to **www.DreamTeamBook.com/behavioralgroundrules**, and **www.DreamTeamBook.com/proceduralgroundrules**.

Ground rules provide important guidance for team operation. They also make it easier for team members to provide feedback to one another. It is less threatening to someone's self esteem to hear, "We all agreed that we will start our meetings on time. But you've been at least 10 minutes late for the past three meetings. I really need you to live up to the agreement we all made to be here on time," then it is to hear "You never show up on time. If you don't care about this team, you shouldn't be on it." You get the idea.

COMMON SENSE POINT

Ground rules help a team work together better. They facilitate feedback among team members. Pointing out when a member acts in a manner that is not consistent with a ground rule is a non-threatening way of providing feedback to one another.

The next component of team infrastructure is **leadership**.

In some teams, like <u>leadership teams</u> and <u>work teams</u>, the leader is apparent – he or she is the person to whom the rest of the team members report … or someone appointed by a senior manager to coordinate the group's activities. In other teams – usually <u>cross function teams</u> or <u>problem solving teams</u> – the group might decide on its own who will handle team leadership responsibilities.

Regardless of how the leader is designated – appointed or chosen by team members – team leadership should be a negotiated process involving feedback and communication. The team should have a voice on what it wants and needs from the leader. And, the leader should be very clear on his or her requirements of team members. This is best accomplished through a conversation in which the leader and members say what they are expecting of one another. If there are significant disagreements about these expectations, the team needs to take the time to engage in a discussion in which these disagreements are explored and resolved.

COMMON SENSE POINT

The role of the team leader needs to be clear and unambiguous. Dream teams take the time to negotiate leadership style.

Finally, there are several **roles and** accompanying **responsibilities** that are present in any successful team, to include …

- Convening the group
- Note taking
- Minutes recording
- Time keeping
- Meeting facilitation and management
- Audio/Visual coordination
- Food/refreshment coordination
- etc.

I've seen some successful teams in which the team leader played all of these roles. I've seen others where these roles were divided among the various members. And, some in which these roles rotated meeting by meeting, or month by month.

The important point here is to realize that there are a number of roles necessary for a team to succeed. It doesn't matter to whom these roles are assigned, but it is important for the team to discuss the various roles it will need to be filled if it is going to succeed – and then to consciously decide who will fill these roles.

COMMON SENSE POINT

Dream teams share the roles that are necessary for team success.

Trust

Team trust is based on three keys:

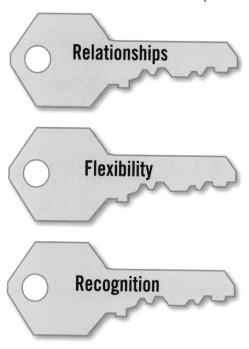

Trust begins with **relationships**. Many people ask me how I market. I tell them I market by building relationships with others – often helping them and asking for nothing in return. Why do I do this? Because I've discovered a few important truisms about human interaction:

> *People who like me are more likely to be willing to be in a relationship with me.*
>
> *People who are in a relationship with me are more likely to trust me.*
>
> *People who trust me are more likely to want to do business with me.*

It's just that simple. And the same is true for teams.

In most cases, members of high performing teams really like one another. And, they like *being with* one another. They build and maintain relationships they go beyond work. These relationships lead to the trust necessary for teams to get through the inevitable "bumps" that occur as they work on tasks and activities.

When I am asked to facilitate a new team, I always begin by spending a fair bit of time helping team members get to know each other as people. This involves more than the usual, "Hi, I'm Bud. I live in Denver and run my own business." I ask people to provide that information, but I also ask them to share things with the team that they normally might not reveal to business colleagues.

As I begin these discussions, some people are either uncomfortable with such conversation, or clearly think it is a waste of time. Usually these same people will come up to me afterwards and say that they really got a lot out of these introductions and feel more comfortable being on the team because they know, understand, and can relate to the other members much better.

> The most important single ingredient in the formula of success is knowing how to get along with people.
>
> — THEODORE ROOSEVELT

Isaiah Thomas was a high profile NBA player in 2002. However, he was not selected for the Olympic Dream Team because many of the other team members didn't like him. In fact, some said that they would refuse to play if Isaiah were selected.

Chuck Daly, the coach of the Dream Team, and Isaiah's coach on the Detroit Pistons, chose to leave him off of the team. Coach Daly was concerned that selecting Thomas would be a detriment to the team's "chemistry."

Judging by his masterful performance on the basketball court, Isaiah Thomas should have been selected for the Dream Team. However, his relationships with most of the other players was so strained that – despite his talent – he was not asked to participate. Fair? Maybe, maybe not. Good for the team? Absolutely!

COMMON SENSE POINT

People work better together when they take the time to build relationships with other team members. Dream team members are comfortable with, and really like, one another.

Flexibility is the second key to building team trust.

When you're flexible, you're willing to subordinate your point of view in the interest of helping the team move forward. This doesn't mean that you should be a milquetoast and never stand up for your ideas. It does mean, however, that you should be willing to go along with the majority opinion and support the team's wishes – especially when the matter under discussion is not something about which you feel strongly.

When you're flexible, you make big deposits into the emotional bank accounts you have with your teammates. These deposits will come in handy if you ever feel the need to make a "withdrawal" … to take a stand and hold firm on one of your ideas.

By demonstrating flexibility, you earn the right to expect the same from your fellow team members. And you earn their trust as they see that you truly are interested in what's best for everyone rather than merely advancing your own agenda.

COMMON SENSE POINT

On effective teams, people are willing to give in on
small points of disagreement for the benefit of the team.

The last key to trust is **recognition**. Over the years, I've learned that one of the very best ways to build trust is to give your teammates a pat on the back for a job well done. Just about everyone likes it when someone recognizes them for what they've done. Don't you?

There are all sorts of things for which you can recognize your teammates: a good idea, a clear set of minutes, supporting your point of view, volunteering to take the lead on a sub team, etc. The list is practically endless. And recognizing others is easy. All it takes is saying,

> *You did a great job on XXX, and I just want you*
> *to know that I really appreciate it.*

When you do this, you are not only building a stronger relationship with that person, you're gaining their trust. People trust others who are kind to them. It's a natural human reaction. But, most of us are a little out of practice when it comes to expressing our sincere appreciation to others. And that's too bad.

So here's what I suggest: Actively look for ways to recognize the people in your life. "Catch" them doing something right and tell them about it. You'll feel better for having done it – and you will make yet another deposit in your emotional trust bank account with him or her.

COMMON SENSE POINT

People trust those who take a minute or two to recognize them for what they do. Look for opportunities to recognize your teammates and reinforce them for helping the team.

Spirit

Spirit is the final internal factor important to creating a dream team.

Team spirit is characterized by three things:

The best teams have members who are proud and excited to be a part of the group. They are honored by their inclusion on the team and enthusiastic about the contributions they can make to both the team and the larger organization.

This sense of **pride** and **excitement** typically leads to greater **mutual accountability**. In the best teams, members realize that they are part of something bigger than themselves. They don't want to disappoint their teammates. They raise their level of performance to make sure that the team succeeds.

> Pride is a personal commitment. It is an attitude which separates excellence from mediocrity.
>
> — UNKNOWN

Think about the original Dream Team. These guys were all celebrities. Multi-millionaires. Yet, they played with a sense of pride, excitement and mutual accountability. There were a lot of very good professional basketball players who did not go to those Olympics. The ones who did were very proud to be on the team. They played with a ferocity that demonstrated a true sense of personal pride.

The original Dream Team was like a bunch of little kids after they won the gold medal. I've seldom seen grown men so happy about winning a sporting event. They had tons of pride and generated excitement wherever they went. And, they were mutually accountable. They played as one. These were the biggest stars on their teams. Yet, for those eight games, they were all dedicated to one goal – winning the Olympic Gold Medal – and doing it in convincing fashion.

Take a lesson from that first Dream Team. Create a sense of pride and excitement among team members. Get them to put aside their individual differences, and organizational differences. Get them pulling together as one.

COMMON SENSE POINT

Dream teams work as one. Members are proud and excited to be on the team. They work well together because they don't want to disappoint the other members of the team.

Relationships with External Constituencies

No team exists in a vacuum. External relationships are an often over-looked factor of team success. Dream Teams manage their external relationships with just as much care as they manage internal ones.

Managing external team relationships involves …

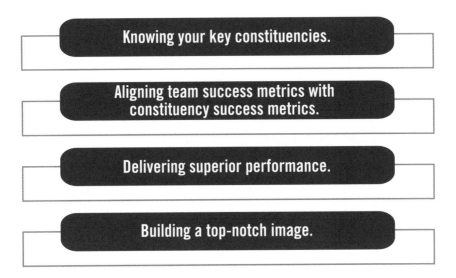

Knowing your key constituencies.

Aligning team success metrics with constituency success metrics.

Delivering superior performance.

Building a top-notch image.

Dream teams begin the process of building and managing relationships by identifying their key constituencies (i.e. "customers"). Different types of teams will have different constituencies.

For example, <u>leadership teams</u> have at least two constituencies: 1) the person or persons to whom they report, and 2) the people they lead in their units or departments. <u>Work team</u> constituencies might include the person to whom they report, and other work teams with whom they interact.

<u>Cross function</u> teams are usually created to enhance communication and cooperation among different work groups. This means that each work group that is represented on the team is a constituency – along with the leadership of the operation. Finally, the person or team who chartered a <u>project team</u> is the main constituency of that team.

Effective teams identify and understand their constituencies by asking questions such as:

Which groups have a stake in the outcome of our work?

What are they hoping/expecting that we will achieve?

Who are the important people in these groups?

What metrics will they use to measure our success?

The answers to these questions provide valuable information that will keep the team moving in the right direction. You have to know what your key constituencies are expecting of you if you are going to be able to deliver what they want.

COMMON SENSE POINT

Dream teams identify their key constituency groups
and the key people in each of those groups.

The second step is to align the team's success metrics with the success metrics of the external constituencies. Here's an example …

Several years ago, I was doing some consulting work for a company that mined talc. The mine, itself, was in rural Montana. And, trust me, shipping can be a problem when you are located in rural Montana – especially during the winter months. Trains and trucks just don't move the same as they do in nicer weather.

This company, which prided itself on providing great customer service, was unpleasantly surprised by a recent customer survey – receiving very low marks for on-time delivery. At first, they were puzzled. They didn't understand these low ratings since they had made every one of their ship dates. I was facilitating a leadership team meeting to address this problem. I listened for a few minutes and then asked, "What is your measure of success here?" They said, "Ship date." Then I asked, "What is your customers' measure of success?" They thought for a minute, and then one team member uttered, "Probably, *delivery* date." This was an "aha moment." Members of this team figured out that their internal metrics were not aligned with the metrics of one of their most important constituencies – their customers.

The team fixed this problem in a very simple way – they pushed their promised delivery dates back by a week and never again missed making an on time delivery.

COMMON SENSE POINT

Dream teams align their internal success metrics with the success metrics of their key constituencies.

The third step is to perform … you have to meet or beat the aligned success metrics. To illustrate this, let's look at a product management marketing team, a sales team, and sales aids.

Sales aids (charts, graphs, a/v presentations, etc.) are often the output of a product management marketing team. Members of sales teams who actually use them expect these aids to be clear, concise, easy to work with, error free, and accurate. But that's certainly not always the case. Not too long ago, a sales professional showed me an aid that was a PowerPoint presentation with several build slides and links built into it. She complained that the presentation was difficult to use because she can't always get on line at customers' locations to use the links. When I mentioned this to the product marketing manager, he said that the build slides enhance the aesthetics of the presentation, and that the links were there only if the sales person needed further back up to what she was saying in the presentation.

Unfortunately, in this case there were two types of disconnects – one in not agreed upon success metrics and the other in performance. The sales person wanted ease of use. The product manager and his team were more interested in aesthetics of the presentation. The output of the product marketing team – the sales aids – did not meet the needs of the sales team. Hence, the sales team, a key constituent, felt that the product management team was performing poorly.

COMMON SENSE POINT

Dream teams are high performing.
They over deliver on their promises.

The fourth step is to build a strong, professional team image in the eyes of your key constituencies.

Make sure the people you're serving are aware of your team's performance. Keep them in the loop let them know when you have achieved major milestones. Make sure they know that you understand their needs and issues – and that you are committed to doing everything you can to exceed their expectations.

Invite your constituencies to attend your team planning meetings. Offer to make a presentation at one of *their* meetings. Keep in touch with them … ask them to join you for lunch or for a cup of coffee.

You see, it works like this: The more you communicate and interact with your constituencies, the more you will understand their needs and issues. The more you understand their needs and issues, the easier it will be for you to address them. And, the more you address their needs and issues, the more your constituencies will see your group as a top-notch team.

COMMON SENSE POINT

Dream teams treat their team as a "brand." They constantly and consistently promote the team to their constituencies.

Things You'll Observe in a
DREAM TEAM

- Team members share participation equally.

- Team members listen to one another.

- Team members express their thoughts and feelings openly.

- Team members support and encourage one another.

- Team members follow an agreed upon decision making process.

- Alternative solutions are raised and discussed completely.

- Decisions are reached by consensus.

- All team members accept and commit to team decisions.

- The team develops actions plans to implement decisions.

- All team members take responsibility for those action plans.

- Members focus on the tasks and the processes of the team.

- Leadership is negotiated by team members.

- Conflict is dealt with by searching for common ground and creative solutions.

- Conflict focuses on ideas, not personalities.

- There are well defined norms of behavior that all members follow.

- Team members confront one another when behavior falls outside of defined team norms.

- The team occasionally reviews and modifies norms as necessary.

- The team environment is *calm, warm, energetic, involved, close, confident, competent, productive, trusting, open, supportive* and *innovative.*

Bonus Common Sense:
Conducting Team Meetings

Teams and meetings ... meetings and teams. The two are literally inseparable. Teams use meetings – whether face to face or virtual – to accomplish their work. Here is a checklist with some bonus common sense advice on how to plan for and conduct productive, effective team meetings.

Before the Meeting – Prepare

Answer these questions:

- What needs to be accomplished?

- Who needs to be in attendance?

- When is the best time for the meeting?

- Where is the best place for the meeting?

Develop an agenda by listing the topics to be covered in the meeting. For each topic, answer the following questions:

- How much time is required?

- What is the expected outcome (e.g., information sharing, decision, etc.)?

- What information or material on this topic should participants bring with them to the meeting?

- How should participants prepare for this topic (i.e., what should they read, review, etc.)?

During the Meeting – Control the Discussion

- Some people may need to vent ... let them.
  This helps people calm down, relax, and concentrate.

- Avoid taking sides in disputes.
  Mediate disagreements – point out the valid points on each side of the argument.

- Involve everybody in solving disputes.
  Bring in other people – especially those not involved in the dispute.

- Focus on facts, not opinions.
  Ask specific questions (i.e. "How many times has this happened?").

- Stay alert – keep the discussion on the point.
  Listen with an open mind.
  Keep notes of the key points.
  Stop people from going over old ground.
  Stop people from jumping to conclusions.
  Ask yourself, "Is this discussion relevant to the issue?"

- If the discussion begins to veer off track, make course corrections early.

  Be polite, but firm – It's okay to say, "That's interesting, but it's not what we're here to discuss."
  Talk to the people who regularly take meetings off on a tangent. Ask for their help in sticking to the topic.

- Check for understanding.

  Ask questions for clarification.

  Check your assumptions – make sure you really hear what everyone is saying. If you don't understand something, others may be confused as well.

  Paraphrase decisions – make sure everyone is clear.

- Don't make decisions too quickly.

  Avoid "squashing" ideas prematurely.

  Avoid jumping to conclusions.

  Make sure everyone has a chance to be heard.

  Control dominant personalities – probe quiet ones.

  Don't allow ridiculing of people or their ideas.

- Record all ideas and suggestions on a flip chart.

  Consider appointing a "scribe" to do the writing.

  Ask people, by name, for their thoughts and input.

  Periodically review your flip-chart lists.

- Build on ideas.

  Ask specific questions (i.e. "How many times has this happened?").

  Use as many ideas, or parts of them, as you can.

  Look for something positive in every idea.

  Find ways to "piggyback" on ideas.

  Acknowledge and thank people for their input.

Ending the Meeting – Review and Thanks

- Summarize discussion points and decisions made.

- Review actions items – "What happens next?"
  Clarify what will happen after the meeting.
  Describe what will be done – when and by whom.
  Paraphrase decisions – make sure everyone is clear.

- Set the date, time, and location of the next meeting (if applicable).

- Thank everyone for their time, their participation, and their contributions.

After the Meeting – Follow-up

- Distribute written "minutes" of the meeting to all participants.

- Monitor progress on action items.
  Check, periodically, to make sure people are on track and on schedule.

- Use action items to begin agenda development for the next meeting(s).

Summary

There you have it – a collection of common sense ideas and strategies to help you create your own high-performing DREAM TEAM:

- Establish a clear purpose or charter for the team.
- Manage the internal factors:

    Create an infrastructure that works for you.

    Actively build trust among team members.

    Promote a team spirit that encourages pride, excitement and mutual accountability.

- Build and maintain strong relationships with important outside constituencies:

    Determine their wants and needs and how they will measure team success.

    Align the team's success metrics with constituency metrics.

    Perform; do better than the metrics.

    Build the team's image by keeping constituents informed of your progress.

Remember that teams are powerful … teams are greater than the sum of their parts … teams are the manifestation of a strong commitment to inclusiveness and engagement.

When you build and manage them right, TEAMS WORK!

"I am a member of a team,
and I rely on the team,
I defer to it and sacrifice for it
because the team, not the individual,
is the ultimate champion."

— MIA HAMM

About the Author

Bud Bilanich, "The Common Sense Guy," is a success coach, motivational speaker, author and blogger. He helps individuals, teams and entire organizations succeed by applying their common sense.

Dr. Bilanich is Harvard educated but has a no-nonsense approach to his work that goes back to his roots in the steel country of Western Pennsylvania. In addition to *Common Sense Ideas for Building a Dream Team*, Bud is the author of eleven books including three Walk the Talk publications:

Your Success GPS

Leading With Values

Solving Performance Problems

His clients include Pfizer, Glaxo SmithKline, Johnson and Johnson, Abbot Laboratories, PepsiCo, AT&T, Chase Manhattan Bank, Citigroup, General Motors, UBS, AXA Advisors, Cabot Corporation, Aetna, PECO Energy, Olin Corporation, Minerals Technologies, The Boys and Girls Clubs of America and a number of small and family owned businesses.

Dr. Bilanich received an Ed.D from Harvard University, an MA from the University of Colorado, and a BS from Penn State.

He is a cancer survivor and lives in Denver, Colorado with his wife, Cathy. Bud is a retired rugby player, an avid cyclist, and a Penn State and Pittsburgh Steelers football fan. He enjoys independent films, live theatre, and crime fiction.

ABOUT WalkTheTalk.Com

For over 30 years, WalkTheTalk.com has been dedicated to one simple goal…one single mission: *To provide you and your organization with high-impact resources for your personal and professional success.*

Walk The Talk resources are designed to:

- Develop your skills and confidence
- Inspire your team
- Create customer enthusiasm
- Build leadership skills
- Stretch your mind
- Handle tough "people problems"
- Develop a culture of respect and responsibility
- And, most importantly, help you achieve your personal and professional goals.

Visit WalkTheTalk.com to learn more about our:

Leadership and Employee Development Centre

- Develop your Leaders
- Build Employee Commitment
- Achieve Business Results

Free Newsletters

- Daily Inspiration
- The Power of Inspiration
- The Leadership Solution
- Inspired Living

Motivational Gift Books

- Inspire your Team
- Create Customer Enthusiasm
- Reinforce Core Values